B53 004 407 6

KT-523-586

Flip the Flaps

Minibeasts

Karen Wallace and Tudor Humphries

KINGFISHER

KINGFISHER

First published 2008 by Kingfisher
This edition published 2012 by Kingfisher
an imprint of Macmillan Children's Books
a division of Macmillan Publishers Limited
20 New Wharf Road, London N1 9RR
Basingstoke and Oxford
Associated companies throughout the world
www.panmacmillan.com

Consultant: David Burnie

ISBN 978-0-7534-3398-0

Copyright © Macmillan Children's Books 2008

All rights reserved. No part of this publication may be reproduced,
stored in or introduced into a retrieval system, or transmitted, in any
form or by any means (electronic, mechanical, photocopying,
recording or otherwise), without prior written permission of the
publisher. Any person who does any unauthorized act in
relation to this publication may be liable to criminal
prosecution and civil claims for damages.

2 4 6 8 9 7 5 3 1
1TR/0911/UNTD/LFA/157MA

A CIP record is available from the British Library.

Printed in China

This book is sold subject to the condition that it shall not, by way
of trade or otherwise be lent, resold, hired out, or otherwise circulated
without the publisher's prior consent in any form of binding or cover
other than that in which it is published and without a similar condition
including this condition being imposed on the subsequent purchaser.

ROTHERHAM LIBRARY SERVICE	
B53004407	
Bertrams	30/12/2011
JN	£5.99
CLS	J595.7

Contents

What are minibeasts?

Minibeasts are tiny animals, such as insects and spiders. They have been on Earth for millions of years and live in all sorts of different places, from hot, wet jungles to cold, rocky mountains.

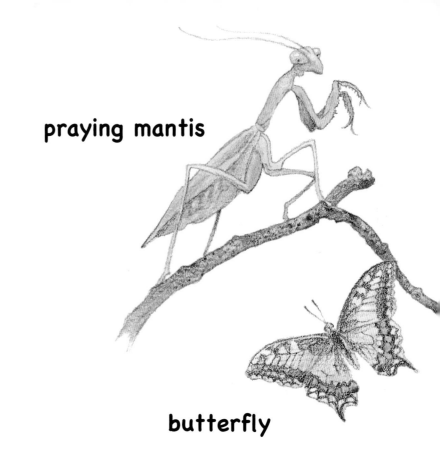

praying mantis

butterfly

two male stag beetles

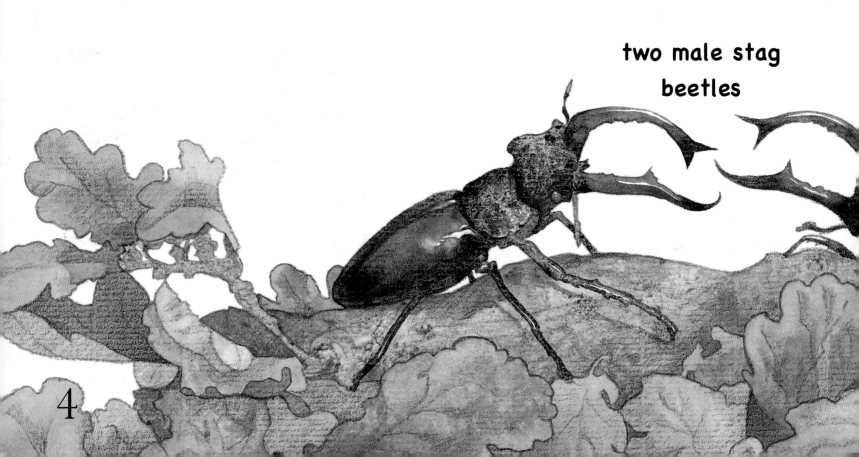

4

1. All insects have six legs. They also have three parts to their body – a head, thorax and abdomen.

2. There are millions of types of insect. They come in different shapes, colours and sizes.

3. Yes. Beetles are insects. Some are very colourful; others have huge jaws.

A stag beetle attacks another with its jaws.

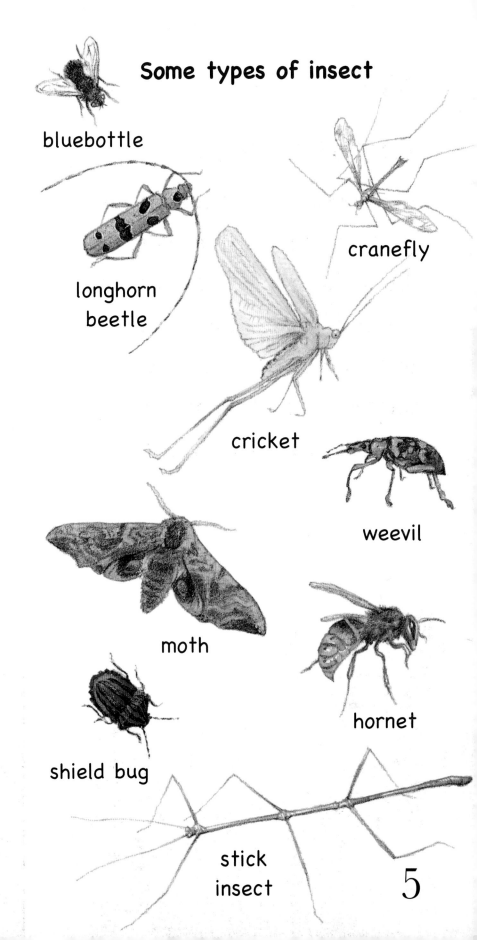

Some types of insect

bluebottle

longhorn beetle

cranefly

cricket

weevil

moth

shield bug

hornet

stick insect

5

Ladybirds

Ladybirds are small beetles with wings. They are easy to see because they have colourful, spotted shells. Ladybirds live in gardens and meadows, and have tiny mouths and a pair of jaws.

ladybird on a leaf

ladybirds on flowers

6

1. How do ladybirds smell, taste and feel?

2. Can a ladybird fly?

ect

3. What does a ladybird eat?

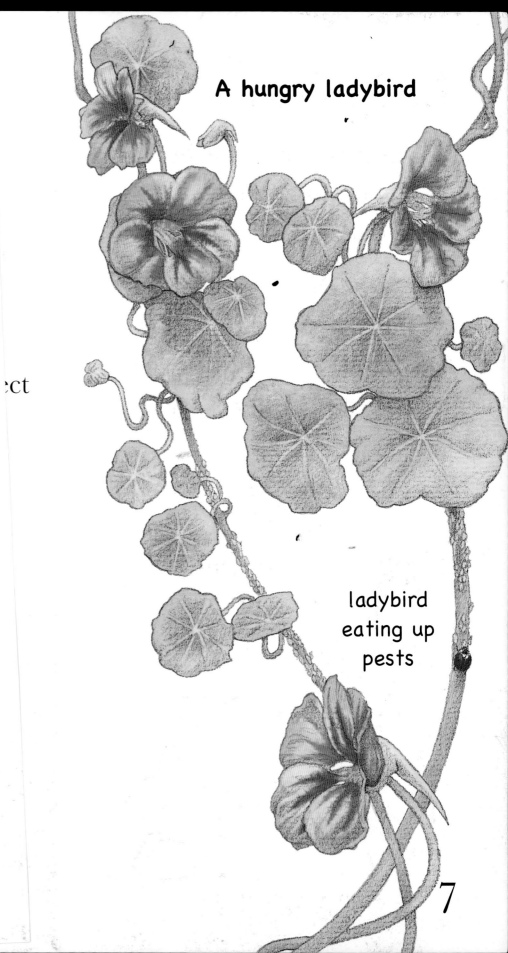

A hungry ladybird

ladybird eating up pests

7

Ants

Ants are busy insects that live in large groups. Some make their nests under stones, in the ground, or inside logs or trees. Wood ants make their nests inside a giant pile of dead leaves.

queen ant flying

wood ants' nest

1. Can any ants fly?

2. How many ants
   live in a nest?

3. Why do some ants
   cut up leaves?

y
lose
nd.

n

aws.

l.

Leaf-cutter ants

Butterflies

There are many types of butterfly. Some of them fly a long way to spend winter in warm sunshine. Most butterflies feed on flowers. They suck up their food through a long, hollow mouth.

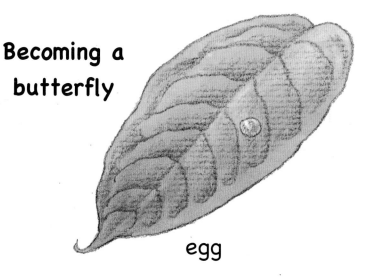

Becoming a butterfly

egg

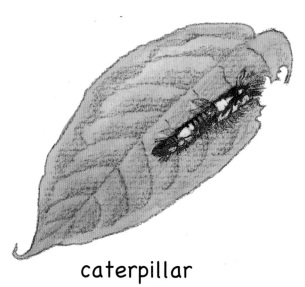

caterpillar

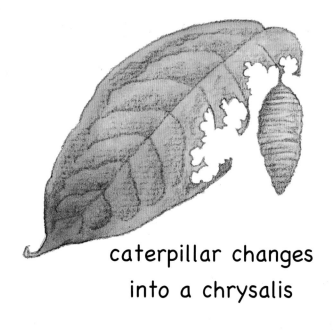

caterpillar changes into a chrysalis

butterfly on a flower

mouth curled up

10

1. How many eggs do butterflies lay?

2. How does a caterpillar turn into a butterfly?

3. Which butterfly has extra-strong wings?

Monarch butterflies flying south in the winter

Spiders

There are over 40,000 different types of spider. They can be smaller than a tip of a pencil or bigger than a dinner plate. All spiders can grow a new leg if one breaks.

Mexican redknee tarantula

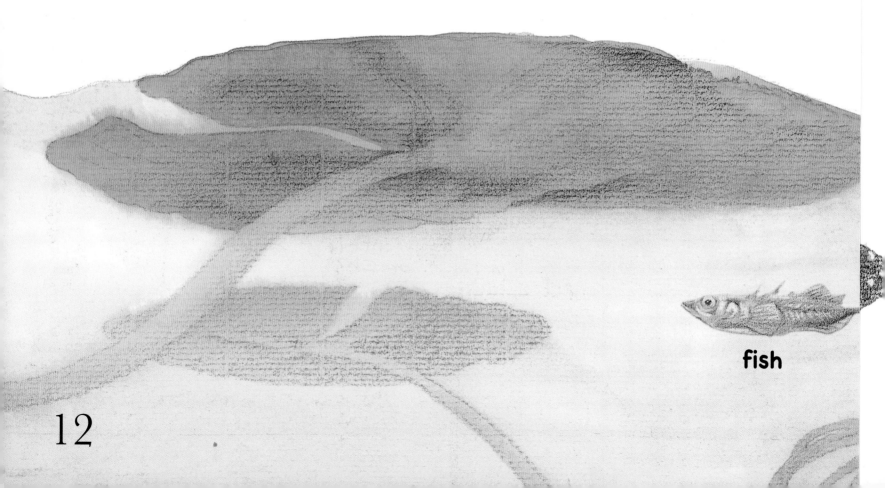

fish

12

1. Do all spiders live on webs?

2. How does a spider build a web?

3. Why do water spiders have long, hairy legs?

water spider in its air bubble nest

Building a web

building lines of silk

the web is finished

Honeybees

Honeybees make their nests from wax. Inside the nest, there are thousands of small spaces, called cells. Some cells are used to store honey, and the queen bee lays her eggs in others.

honeybee nest

honeybees flying

14

1. How do honeybees talk to each other?

2. How do honeybees make honey?

3. What keeps a queen bee busy in spring?

t special
er bees
e the
growing.

nectar, a
m flowers.
to honey
es.

en
two
day.

queen honeybee
laying eggs

worker honeybee
feeding a grub
(baby bee)

young
honeybee
climbing
out of a cell

15

Dragonflies

Dragonflies live by ponds and lakes. They are speedy hunters that feed on smaller insects. Some hover in the air and chase after their food. Others lie in wait, snatching up insects that come too close.

dragonfly

ee dancing

oneybee
king nectar

Once, dragonflies were huge.

16

1. Do dragonflies
have eyes?

2. Why do dragonflies
have four wings?

3. How long have
dragonflies lived
on Earth?

eye

dragonfly

Dragonflies are
smaller today.

1. Dragonflies have the largest eyes of all insects.

hungry toad lying in wait

2. Dragonflies can move their wings in different directions. They can fly forwards or backwards to escape danger.

3. Dragonflies have lived on Earth for 300 million years. They were around even before the dinosaurs!

dragonfly flying backwards

Index